Beyond Design: Complete Kitchens

KRISTA PIPPY

Beyond Design: Complete Kitchens Copyright © Krista Pippy 2019.

All rights reserved. No part of this publication may be reproduced, distributed or transmitted in any form or by any means, including photocopying, recording, or other electronic or mechanical methods, without the prior written permission of the author or publisher, except in the case of brief quotations embodied in critical reviews and certain other noncommercial uses permitted by copyright law.

Disclaimer: Some names and identifying details have been changed to protect the privacy of individuals.

Published by Prominence Publishing. www.prominencepublishing.com

To contact the author, email: krista_pippy@hotmail.com.

Publisher's Note: This is for educational and entertainment purposes only. This is not meant to represent legal, medical, or any other kind of professional advice. The reader should do his or her own due diligence and seek professional advice when required.

Beyond Design: Complete Kitchens / Krista Pippy. -- 1st ed.

ISBN: 978-1-988925-42-4

Cover photo credit: Gillian Fisher.

Design of the kitchen on the cover:
Jennifer Power & Stacy Williams of Instyle Interiors.

To Makayla and Amber my two precious daughters, who make me strive to be a better person and enrich my life beyond measure.

To my family, friends, co-workers and clients that have been by my side every step of the way.

And to the woman that inspires me every day with her support and love, my mom, Olga Pippy. Thanks for everything!

Table of Contents

Foreword 7

Chapter One: Style 11

Chapter Two: Personalize Your Kitchen
    For You and Your Family 25

Chapter Three: Renovating Your Kitchen
    vs. Building a New Home 33

Chapter Four: Frequently Asked Questions 39

Chapter Five: Your Budget 49

Chapter Six: Universal Design 53

Chapter Seven: Specialty Features for Kitchens 57

Chapter Eight: Countertop Options 71

Chapter Nine: Appliances 77

Chapter Ten: Finishing Touches 83

Chapter Eleven: How to Choose a Designer 89

Checklists 93

What People Are Saying About Krista Pippy 98

About the Author, Krista Pippy 102

Foreword

It was the spring of 2017 when I first met Krista at a Canadian Kitchen Cabinet Conference in Halifax. We bonded over how she paired a cute jean jacket with yoga pants, as I envied her sense of style. The company I worked for at the time sponsored an axe throwing event, complete with drinks and real axes (sounds like a bad idea), and encouraged everyone to wear plaid. When Krista came in voluntarily wearing plaid while I begrudged my forced plaid outfit and matching beard, (don't ask), I knew this girl was amazing. Have you ever met a Newfoundlander that wasn't?

And the rest is history. We've partnered together on other ventures, and taken trips to Edmonton and Vegas.

When it came time to design my kitchen in my new 'forever' house I thought the kitchen would be the easiest part. After all, I've been working in the cabinet manufacturing industry for over 20 years, starting in the drafting and design department, then moving to operating the machines, programming, and eventually project management. I handled big projects like hospitals, hotels, and grocery stores, so I figured this 10' x 9' kitchen would be a breeze!

What I quickly found out was that I knew too much! I had seen all these fun and cool things over the years and wanted it all! But I just couldn't make it all work the way I wanted it to. I had my list of non-negotiables, and my 'nice to have' items, but kept getting lost in the rabbit hole of the internet looking at all kinds of inspirational photos. After months of revising and redrawing, it was getting close to the time we needed to get the kitchen ordered so I didn't hold up the project. I finally gave in and asked Krista to give it a second set of eyes. She flipped it around in a way I had not thought of, giving me a big island, as well as some seasonal cabinets and saved me money by turning my pantry to the side!

Now if I was having trouble designing my kitchen, even with over 20+ years' experience in the industry, how is the average homeowner supposed to do it by themselves? The kitchen will be one of the highest valued areas in your home and by far the most utilized.

When Krista told me she was writing this book, I had two thoughts: 1. Brilliant! I spend a lot of time helping my friends make heads or tails of their kitchen designs, and communications so this will be helpful, and 2. Where was this book when I needed it?

This book is so well laid out. It covers everything from budgeting, design elements and explanations of the different decisions you'll need to consider. Picking a kitchen from a photo isn't enough. This book will guide you through deciding what your personal style is, how your family functions daily and how you can make your kitchen look amazing but also be functional. It is your guide to everything kitchens.

We've been in our home for 2 years, and we've only used our kitchen table twice. We are a family of busy entrepreneurs; our kitchen has become the place to be where we can chat about our day while prepping meals. When we have gatherings, everyone gravitates to our kitchen because it's so functional, open and inviting. A good old fashioned Maritime kitchen party. Thanks to Krista, we have a much needed bigger island!

Take the time to read this book and enjoy your new kitchen for years to come!

Michelle Hoy
Clear Build Solutions
Bonshaw, PEI, August 8, 2019

CHAPTER ONE

Style

> " What does your kitchen say about you? What's your kitchen style? "

The kitchen is one of the most significant rooms in your home; that's why people refer to the kitchen as "the heart of your home." It's the general room of every get-together, cook-off and lazy Sunday. It's not just where the food and refreshments are — the kitchen is the central hub that runs a family. It's typically the single most important room in a house and it says a lot about who you are. So when you consider the design of your kitchen, the layout and functionality it should reflect your needs, personality, and lifestyle.

You can learn a lot about a person by taking a step inside their kitchen. As the heart of the home, the kitchen is also one of the most descriptive rooms in the house. Your kitchen signifies more about your wants, needs, and daily habits than you might think.

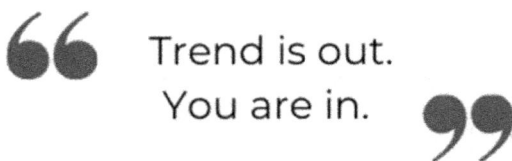

Trend is out. You are in.

Personal style should be your main focus when designing your kitchen, not just in the way it looks but in the way it feels when you use it. Whatever inspires you, bring those elements into your kitchen design. Forget about making it look picture perfect at the moment. Rather, think about how you can include your personality into your kitchen?

The simplest way to add character into your kitchen space is to use artwork and accessories. Items that are extremely personal to you will help transform your kitchen into a space that reflects you and your personal style. A great piece of artwork will provide an interesting focal point in your kitchen. Skillfully matching kitchen accessories in similar colors to your artwork will bring explosions of color and a beautiful sense of flow.

Make the style your own by thinking a little bit of what does and does not express your taste. There is no shortage of ideas out there, but finding the right place to start for your specific kitchen can be a bit overwhelming. Here are some kitchen styles that may appeal to you.

Country farmhouse

Are you the romantic among us and love those tear-jerkers? If this is you, then a Country Farm House Kitchen might be what you're looking for.

The country kitchen is very easy to love and is your ultimate comfort zone. It's got to be comfy, embracing and full of all the delicious treats you can imagine.

This style is set apart by the use of different textures, open beams, butcher block countertops, and painted historic colour finishes mixed with wood. An apron style sink is something that really adds to a country feel, while open cabinets and very ornate touches like chunky legs on your island gives that old time charm.

Traditional

Are you a lover of 18th-century form where the cultural customs of dining were the focus of the meal or are you the pinnacle of all styles, before and after? If this is your personality then a traditional kitchen will give you a connection to history, comfort and neatness.

Don't confuse a traditional kitchen with a Country Farm House style. A traditional kitchen design style is "welcoming and timeless" and traditional kitchens incorporate soft color schemes such as cream, white, taupe, light gray, blue or green.

Part of its attraction, like country, is that it brings the outdoors in, so you can mix and match different woods, fabrics, metals and textures. It's a design that appeals to the masses.

Modern

Are you not one to dwell in the past, but you certainly learn from it? Do you consider yourself more of a scientist than a cook? If so, a modern kitchen is probably what you are looking for. This kitchen style is your universe, and your creations are as exciting as you are, with the same impulsive charm.

In the present era, modern kitchen design is part of a bigger trend which has embraced midcentury design. Modern kitchen design is generally categorized as any style that's less traditional and more contemporary. Modern kitchen designs feature flat surfaces and geometric forms. The most important rules in a modern kitchen are no extraneous elements, no raised panels, and no extra moldings. They often feature man-made materials like laminate, ceramics and molded plastics.

Gas ranges and multiple ovens, standalone fridges and freezers make for a very sleek look and modern design.

Most people think of a slab cabinet door style when they think modern but you can use a simple shaker style and achieve the same modern feel.

Contemporary

Are you a minimalist and artistic by nature?

Contemporary kitchens are one of the most admired styles of kitchen, and for a good reason. They're clean, stylish and uncluttered – while still remaining functional and practical.

> When it comes to designing or renovating a kitchen, most people are not sure where to start.

Contemporary kitchens have a sleek, simple layout characterized by dark wood or black cabinetry, crisp white countertops and slick stainless steel appliances; the contemporary kitchen is practical and simplistic.

Keeping countertop clutters to a minimum by choosing space-saving innovations to store smaller appliances and accessories such as pot and pan drawers, spice pulls, toe kick drawers and appliance lifts they can fit into almost any sized kitchen area.

The contemporary design also gives you the illusion of a larger kitchen by using clean horizontal lines and frameless cabinets giving more of a seamless design.

Transitional

Are you a mixture of all of the above personalities? If so, the transitional kitchen is for you! Almost everything is up for discussion when designing a transitional kitchen.

Transitional kitchens are a combination of traditional and contemporary kitchen styles, often using clean lines while also throwing in some traditional design. Transitional kitchens work great with most home designs and offer you flexibility.

A transitional kitchen is a highly sought-after look—yet not many people can truly define it, let alone create it. Think of the transitional kitchen as a stylish go-between of the timelessness of traditional design and the clean, simple lines of contemporary style.

Shaker-style kitchen cabinets are a common choice because it is a timeless design that mixes well into modern and traditional schemes, making it a good option if you are looking for a kitchen that will see you through potential kitchen redesigns

My Dream Kitchen

"A couple of years ago, I was diagnosed with a debilitating disease. I was told I should end a career I dearly loved and retire. Retirement was challenging, simply because my work was a huge part of my life, so I decided to develop some interests and activities I could do at home – I found cooking!

My husband and I made a decision to build a new home to accommodate my illness. One of our challenges was the kitchen – my favorite room in the house. Off I go to collect magazines, pictures, lots of internet searching, and visiting kitchen cabinet businesses for ideas, when in hindsight, I just had to visit Krista Pippy and her professional staff... and so it began.

After my first conversation, I knew this was a good fit. The staff made this adventurous project all about our needs, especially mine – you see it was not going to be the typical kitchen and 'blue' is my favorite color. Blue – the color of the sea, the color of the sky in sunshine, and a colour of tranquility and peace; some may see it as a negative feeling, 'blue'. I saw it as a feeling of relaxation and a closeness to nature. To my surprise, I got many eye-opening expressions when I voiced that I wanted a blue kitchen, but not Krista – she loved the idea and was eager to take on a new challenge. She was incredibly excited - I became the lady with the blue kitchen!

I was asked to provide something on paper, to give them some ideas of my needs and desires. I was not judged on my poor artistic abilities, I might add! The kitchen was designed with pencil scratches, nothing to scale nor a consideration of building codes, and I was oblivious to the necessary footage, but it was nothing that the professionals couldn't fix! What in the world was I thinking? Oh no, space was something we were not in abundance of. This was an adversity which turned into an opportunity for Krista to shine, "We will make it work!"

Due to my mobility limitations, certain things had to be kept in mind – a need for counter height adjustment and ease of accessibility, just to name a few. The entire lower portion of the kitchen was equipped with easy rolling drawers, a walk-in pantry area, and a minimum number of upper cabinets. The wall oven, wall microwave, and stove top are all at counter height. In addition to my needs, my husband had some wishes – you see, he is the at-home barista, therefore a beverage unit was to be considered as part of the design; we all have our passions! Once again, Krista made it work!

Now, for little things, to make the kitchen unique, rustic in nature and blue in color, oh, did I mention, with a black glaze? Hmmm.... Something for contrast was the next decision, something to make the creation 'pop'! Once again, the ideas started to flow from Krista and her team of professionals, who quickly became my friends. We all decided a white island with black glaze would be the accent that was needed. The backsplash would be a clean crisp absolute white with windows for lots of light, and some black floating shelves would be just the thing to give the kitchen some matching appeal. As the ideas flowed from the staff, I became nervous, excited and enthusiastic, all mixed up as one.

With the cooperation of our home builder, BNJ Home Builders, it was instillation day; "Wow" was the only word that came to mind. My childhood memories of Christmas morning came rushing back, and it was more beautiful than I had envisioned. The blue was so gorgeous, rich, and lush, and the island was just the right amount of contrast. The Nay Sayers to my blue kitchen quickly had a change of thought. The beauty of my kitchen is not the only breathtaking, but the functionality is remarkable. I added a splash of bright red, another of my favorite colors, a small addition of personality!

Thank- you Krista Pippy for making my kitchen dreams become a reality!"

Jennifer and Todd Howse

January 2019

CHAPTER TWO

Personalize Your Kitchen for You and Your Family

Every family is different and personalizing your kitchen to suit the needs of your family will make your kitchen more functional and inviting for all members. The following are some options to consider.

Window seat

Do you have a large family and need to use every square inch of space? Do you entertain a lot and require extra seating? Do you have that awkward nook in the kitchen that you are struggling to incorporate into your design? If you answered yes to any of these questions, then a window seat is just what you are looking for.

Everyone tends to naturally congregate in the kitchen, whether it is standing around the island or pulling a chair up to the kitchen table. So why not take that otherwise wasted space in the kitchen and expand your seating with a window seat?

If you are trying to find the perfect way to build in extra seating in the nook area, then customize a window seat that will hug the corners of the bay area, creating space and function. Adding a pedestal table to your nook will maximize your seating.

Every inch matters when designing a window seat so creating functional cabinets or drawers under the seating area will make a great storage area for the seasonal dishes and bulky appliances that you don't use every day. Try adding a cushion to make the seating more comfortable and warm up the space or to just add a pop of color.

Desk

Some people feel a desk in the kitchen is a thing of the past, but if you create a design that makes the desk fit naturally and not like an afterthought, then it can not only add function, it can also add character.

The key is to ensure that the desk complements the kitchen and blends seamlessly into the design. For example, using the same color cabinets and changing the countertop to a butcher block with wooden shelves above can give the space a look of its own yet still fits into the scheme of the kitchen.

Some of the benefits of having a desk in the kitchen are that it will allow extra storage space for keys, mail or schoolwork and can also house extra outlets for charging phones and electronics.

Coffee station

Are you an extreme coffee lover and enjoy savoring a hot cup of java in the comfort of your own home? If so, why not customize your own exclusive coffee station right in your own kitchen!

Setting aside an area on your kitchen countertop to display your coffee pot or espresso machine is a fantastic way to create that special space to place all your coffee necessities. Adding floating shelves or cabinets above will allow for great storage of mugs, sugar dishes or even a piece of artwork to give a distinctive touch.

Island/table combos

Are you struggling with space in your kitchen and still want to have an island and table? Then why not go with an island and table all in one? A great way to achieve this is to have an island counter on one side and a table built onto the other end.

Combining your island and table is an amazing space saver that can seat a crowd and not use up too much of your space.

You can have an island/table combo designed using many different styles and designs. You could also do a drop down table that allows you to use standard chairs, which gives a formal dining room feel. Another option is to have the island and the table at the same height; this will create a larger countertop surface for entertaining and prepping. If you really want to get custom, consider having the table higher than the island, creating more of a pub style feel.

Bar

Do you love to entertain and socialize with friends over a few drinks? If so, you could bring the fun vibes into the kitchen by customizing a bar for all your needs. There are a few ways to incorporate a bar into your kitchen. For example, how about setting aside an area in the kitchen that you would like to have exclusively for a bar area? Consider including a bar fridge, bar sink, wine racks, glass doors, floating shelves and so on. If you have limited space in the kitchen and are unable to set aside a full section just for a home bar, then the island would be a great place to incorporate some wine racks and a bar fridge. You can also add some stylish stools to the island, creating the perfect space for gatherings.

Customizing for your pet

Those of us that have fur babies know that they are just as much a part of the family as everyone else. Treat your pet like a treasured member of the family by customizing an area just for them. Some ways to do this are to dedicate a drawer for the food and then have a smaller drawer below for the food and water dish so your pet can have a tucked away feeding spot.

Some people use a roll out shelf in the bottom of their pantry for large bulky pet food storage, while another option is to install a roll out garbage and use the bin for food.

If you have a lot of extra room in your kitchen, you can create a custom bed at the end of your island or in a base cabinet. This will keep them out from under your feet and by adding a cushion will create the perfect place for napping.

CHAPTER THREE

Renovating Your Kitchen vs. Building a New Home

It is often hard to choose between building a new home and renovating your existing one because there can be benefits to both. If you are finding it hard to make this decision, I suggest getting quotes for both to help you decide whether to love your home again or build your dream home.

Before you even begin to decide which route to take, I recommend that you sit down with your designer and discuss all your options. Be upfront with them about your wants and needs. Having a plan is so important. It is much easier and more cost-effective to do things a certain way from the beginning because they can be costly to do later. Later changes affect the design as well as the budget. For example, I had a client once who wanted to have windows to the left and right of the stove. I was able to advise the building team from the beginning for window placement and it turned out great. If the homeowner had asked for the windows to be added in later, not only would it have been very expensive, it would not have been centered properly on the wall, throwing off the balance and it would have also completely altered the design.

Renovating

Often clients call looking to have a consultation on a kitchen renovation. Most of the time they just want to see what the cost of renovating is so they can decide if it is better to renovate their existing home or build a new one. If you decide that a renovation is the best option for you then you need to find a renovator that you can trust and who you feel comfortable with. Make sure you get references and ask to see some of their past work (in person if possible, not just photos) so you can make sure the finished product and level of quality is what you are looking for.

Find out what kind of services your renovator can provide you. For example, when I do kitchen designs for a customer, sometimes they are not aware that I can also help with the entire renovation from beginning to end and not just the kitchen. I can help with interior design and work with a team of sub-trades to make the job run as smoothly as possible while staying in a specific timeframe.

Also, you want to make sure your renovator provides you with a detailed contract in writing so you know upfront what you are getting and then there are no surprises along the way. Make sure you ask what the process is if you want to make changes at any point. Generally, it is expensive to change things once the renovation is underway so upfront planning is crucial. Discuss with them the timeframe of the project and how it is going to affect your day to day life; this way you can make an informed decision on if you are going to live in the property during the renovation or if you are going to make other living arrangements for the time being. This is a big investment, so you want to make sure that you are involved in the process as much as possible. Ask your contractor for daily updates and make sure they are easy to get in contact with in case you have any questions or concerns.

How important is your neighbourhood to you?

Do you have a nice mature lot? Do the kids have friends and school close by? If you build a new home, will you be able to stay in the area you are comfortable in?

If you have a great house in the perfect area that is big enough for you and your family, then a renovation is probably all you need to feel happy in your home again. Sometimes just giving your kitchen an update will totally change the way you feel about your home. When renovating an older home, be aware that things are not always as they seem. Sometimes a wall that you want to take down may be load-bearing and you may have to do something more structural to get the design you are looking for. Or when you start taking things apart you may run into mold, old electrical wiring or outdated plumbing that has to be addressed. Once, I renovated a kitchen in my own home and discovered there was no insulation whatsoever and also found a bird's nest in the wall! When you are creating a budget, you have to make sure that you plan for the unexpected. You never know what might pop up.

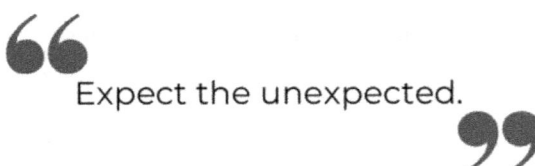

> Expect the unexpected.

There are many different reasons that people choose to renovate a kitchen. Maybe it is an upgrade so that the kitchen can be more functional for their lifestyle. Sometimes it is a renovation to make the house look more up to date or so that you can flip it and make some extra money. Or maybe it is going to be a rental property and you want to make sure you are going to get top dollar for the rent. Whatever your reason, take all of this into consideration when doing a kitchen renovation.

If you are planning on living in the house for a long time and it is going to be your "forever home" and you love the area, then doing a large kitchen Reno or addition will be worth it for you and your family. In this case, moving appliance locations, lighting and walls will not be too much of an inconvenience because you are doing this for the long term. However, if you are renovating the kitchen to flip the house or use as a rental you may want to keep the same footprint and just do a small upgrade to keep the cost down and minimize inconvenience.

Building a new home

When building a brand new home, you can customize it to fit the needs and wants of your family from the inside out. You can choose from a wide variety of floorplans or you can custom design the plan with your builder to make your dream home a reality. During this process you can choose a builder that has a strong reputation and that you feel comfortable dealing with during the building process, providing you with commitment and satisfaction from beginning to end.

When building a home, you are able to see the quality of the construction, ensuring that the materials and products used are durable and provide long term satisfaction. Like a renovation, make sure you get a detailed contract of everything that is included from the building materials to the interior finishes. Most builders will offer you a wide variety of standard choices and also give you a list of upgraded options that may better fit your personality, lifestyle and budget.

With all of the new innovation in home design, you are able to make your new home more energy efficient so you can save money on your day-to-day living expenses which may allow you to have a bigger budget when designing your dream kitchen.

If you are building a new home, you can be more flexible with your layouts and make room to accommodate everything on your kitchen wish list.

It's important to sit with your kitchen designer before your build starts because after reviewing the plan with your designer you may realize that moving a window or wall may make a huge difference in the functionality and design of your kitchen. If you are able to figure this out before the house has been started it is easier to change then and there, rather than waiting until the windows and doors are installed.

CHAPTER FOUR

Frequently Asked Questions

What different materials can be used for kitchens?

You can get many different materials for kitchen cabinets and it can be a bit overwhelming at times. If you are going to go with a stained kitchen you would use a wood species such as birch, maple, oak, walnut, cherry wood, hickory, etc. There are countless stain colors that you can use on the wood but remember different woods are going to take the stain differently. Oak is a wood that has a lot of grain so when you apply the stain the grain is going to be more prominent. Birch and maple are more of a clear wood so you will get less grain when staining them. Birch will take the stain better than maple because it is a softer wood and the stain tends to absorb better. If you put the same stain on a birch and a maple it is going to look lighter on the maple because it is the harder of the two. If you choose a more exotic wood you would normally just do a clear coat to show the beauty of the wood and the grains.

If you are going with a high gloss kitchen then you will have to do a MDF (medium density fiberboard) thermoplastic door. This is a MDF door with a plastic finish that is vacuumed sealed over the door to give you that high gloss plastic look. You can also get these doors in faux wood grain finishes and multiple colors.

If you are planning on going with a painted kitchen it is best to use a MDF door unfinished and then use a lacquer based paint. You can choose any paint color and create any look you like. It's best to use a MDF door when painting your cabinets because it will not shift or cause cracking. Wooden cabinet doors come in 5 pieces that are joined together; when you get different humidity in your home the wood may shrink and expand causing cracking in the finish around the joins and the inside panel.

What are the different types of countertops?

There are many different types of countertops for many different budgets. Laminate countertops would be the most cost-effective and seem to be the counter of choice for most people with a tight budget. Laminate comes in many different colors and profiles.

Granite countertops are a great choice if you are looking for something unique with its natural appeal. The stone from the earth is unsurpassed from almost any other material.

Quartz countertops are an excellent choice when it comes to solid surfaces; it is a 90% stone and 10% man-made material. It is heat resistant, stain resistant and non-porous.

Butcher Block countertops incorporate a warm and inviting feeling into the kitchen. Most people tend to add it to an island, desk, bar, or coffee station.

How far ahead should I plan my kitchen?

It is best to plan your kitchen in advance before you start your new home construction or renovation. It is important to create a wish list and meet with a professional kitchen designer to help with function and placement of appliances, sinks and islands. Planning your kitchen design in the early stages will make it easier for your builder or renovator if changes have to be made such as moving a window or a wall. Providing the kitchen layout in advance allows you to coordinate with sub-trades for any placements or extra features that may need to be added.

How do you make your kitchen trend proof?

White kitchens are very neutral and can act as a backdrop, therefore allowing you to add some modern color on walls and accessories keeping it trendy and easy to change. A shaker door is both modern and traditional therefore standing the test of time.

How to care for your cabinets after install?

The best way to clean your cabinets without causing a reaction to the finish is to use warm water and dish soap with a damp cloth. Avoid using your toaster or kettle under cabinets or countertop joins as the heat and steam will cause water and heat damage to the cabinet finish and possibly delaminate your countertop. Be sure to wipe up any still standing water on countertop joins or on cabinet doors to prevent water damage.

When is the best time to remodel your kitchen?

There is no real ideal time to remodel your kitchen – not everyone's schedule is the same. What is a good time for one person may not be the same for someone else. In my experience most people tend to remodel their kitchen in late spring before the kids get out of school or in the fall just before Christmas. Depending on the extent of the kitchen Reno you have to be prepared to live without a kitchen for a few weeks while all the prep work is being done. If you decide to renovate in the spring and summer months, there will be less mess due to weather and you can BBQ outside instead of eating out at restaurants every night.

How long does a kitchen renovation take?

Cabinet orders take from 4 - 6 weeks. Once all the materials are on site, a starting date will be scheduled. Installation times vary; typically, a kitchen install takes 1 - 2 days depending on the complexity of the project. A more compact kitchen can be installed in as little as a day.

If you choose a solid surface countertop, it can take 4 - 6 weeks after install for the countertops to be templated and installed.

How to choose a designer?

When choosing a designer it is important to make sure you find someone that is open to new ideas and is just as excited about your vision as you are. You want to make sure that they are familiar with industry standards as well as building codes. Make sure you ask for references and you feel comfortable dealing with this person throughout your design process. You are going to want someone that is willing to listen to your ideas and work with you to make your kitchen function for you and your family.

What is your wish list?

Make sure that you create a wish list when getting ready to design your kitchen. Shoot for the stars and then when you sit with your designer you can see what is going to work in your kitchen design and stay within your budget. It is important to make sure you have your list in priority from what is most important to you and your family to what you would like to have but is not that important. For example, if you want to have solid surface countertops and that is a must then you may have to forfeit something else like a wine rack or glass doors so you can stay within your budget. If not, you can think about having solid surface just on the island and laminate countertop on the perimeter so you can have the other little extras and still stay within budget. Not always are you able to incorporate everything on your wish list into your kitchen design, depending on wall space and the floorplan. Try using a checklist when preparing for a kitchen design.

How to make the best use in a small kitchen? (Big Dreams in a small kitchen...)

When designing a small kitchen it is very important to use every bit of space possible. One great way to do this is to extend your kitchen right to the ceiling; this will make the ceiling feel higher and give you an extra shelf in all your upper cabinets for storage. Using toe kick drawers in the small space under the cabinets is great for cookie sheets and cutting boards. Make sure you get rid of visual clutter because having a lot of things on the countertop is going to make the kitchen feel much smaller than it already is. Keeping things organized is a great way to use space in a small kitchen. For example, putting dividers over the fridge, or divide up your drawers for cutlery, utensils or spices. Try picking a design that has clean lines and very minimal design and keep the colour light so the space feels bright. In a small kitchen less is always more!

What are the benefits of a custom kitchen compared to a pre-fabricated kitchen?

A custom kitchen will give you more options for your design and will allow you to utilize every inch of space. There are many different door styles and colours to pick from to fit within every budget. With a pre-fabricated kitchen you are limited to standard sizes not always allowing for a tight fit, in this case you will have to allow for fillers in places causing you to lose space. Once, I had a customer who was renovating some rental properties and as we were chatting, they mentioned that they were just going to go to the boxed store and get cabinets as that would be a cheaper option. After very little convincing, I dropped by their property, took some measurements and got back to them with a design and quote. The price that I gave them was comparable to a boxed store and was a custom made kitchen.

What is a working triangle?

The working triangle is an imaginary line that is 4 - 9 feet between the sink, fridge and stove that is in the shape of a triangle; any less than that and you will not have much room to move around the kitchen. The entire triangle should be 13 - 26 feet for all three sides.

Ideally, there should be nothing interrupting the triangle and no main traffic flow through the triangle; this is not always possible in a smaller home.

How high should a countertop be?

Countertops are usually 36" from the floor in the kitchen and 31" for a desk or drop-down area for a wheelchair. I am often doing the perimeter of the kitchen 36" and then the island 39". If you have a raised eating bar then the raised piece will be 42". You want to customize your kitchen to suit your family and needs so try and get a feel for what you think will work best for you.

How far should my island be away from my appliances?

Industry standards suggest that the island is 42" away from any appliance to give you ample room for moving around. I usually leave the location of the island up to my clients as some people feel that 42" is too much room and they'd rather do a 36" opening around the island. I usually recommend that we get a template of the island and place it onsite and then you can make a more educated decision on where the island works best for your family and space because everyone is different.

What do I need to do to prepare for my kitchen renovation?

It is a good idea to determine what you will be using for an eating and cooking area while your kitchen is under construction. All items need to be removed from the area where construction will take place. Ensure all plugs and switches are moved in the correct location; your designer can indicate where all of this should be positioned.

What will my new kitchen cost?

Remodeling a kitchen is kind of like buying a new car. The base model is thousands cheaper than the loaded model. The more accessories you add, the total price will increase accordingly. You can always use the "Good, Better and Best" options depending on your budget and taste.

Where do I start?

If you are building a new home, email or bring your plans to a professional kitchen designer. If you are remodeling your present kitchen and want some idea what it will cost and what can be done, make an appointment for a designer to drop by and give you a kitchen estimate. Bring in any clippings from magazines of ideas that you like; a picture is worth a thousand words and helps your designer visualize the look you are going for. Based on the information you provide, some price points can be determined. If the figure is more than you expected, don't be disappointed, there are so many design choices to bring the project within your budget. Once you are happy with the pricing and selections, the supplier should come into your home to take final measurements and make any necessary design changes. Once you've made all choices, a perspective drawing will be provided that will give you a very real understanding of how your kitchen will look when completed.

Should I refinish my existing cabinets or purchase new?

From time to time people come to me with this question. But the real question is why are you refinishing? Is it because you just want a little facelift to do you a few years then sell your home or rent it out? Or are you doing this for the long hall and adding solid surface countertops, new hardware and appliances? If you are just doing a little facelift then yes it is probably better to refinish your existing cabinets to freshen up the space and give that updated look you are going for without a huge tear up. If you are planning on staying in the home for many years and investing thousands and thousands of dollars in upgrades then a new kitchen is the best option. The biggest expense of a kitchen is doors, countertop and hardware so it would be a good idea to get quotes for both refinishing and new and compare the two. In my experience the cost difference ends up being very minimal and the customer opts to go new almost every time.

CHAPTER FIVE

Your Budget

A kitchen is no small undertaking so having a budget in mind is essential. Kitchens are the most expensive rooms in the home and also carry additional budgetary demands. Creating the budget and sticking to it can be incredibly difficult. Only 1 in 5 homeowners come in under budget. Always allow for the unexpected — and don't rush decisions.

Choosing a budget

First determine how much you can afford to spend on your new kitchen and ask yourself how long you plan on living in your home. If you intend to stay in your home for 5 years or less then view your kitchen as a return on investment. If you are planning on flipping the house or using it as a rental you may consider lowering your budget. Budget to make sure you spend less than what you will get back on the house. If this is a house you are planning on living in for many years or if this is your "forever home" then allow for a bigger budget so that you are happy and comfortable without worrying about your return on investment. The more detail that's in the proposal, the more likely you'll come in on budget.

You should consider getting at least three quotes before hiring a professional to design your kitchen. When reviewing your quotes make sure you are comparing apples to apples and there is a detailed list of services and materials that are included. Don't forget the "small" costs when doing your budget, they might not seem like much at first, but they can add up very quickly such as upgrading your handles, moldings, glass doors etc.

Understanding the cost breakdown

Usually the biggest part of your budget is your cabinets and labor. Understanding the break down will give you a better idea as to what types of materials to choose to fit your budget. Plan out your project step by step the more itemized your plan, the better prepared you'll be for any unexpected costs that may arise.

Here's an example of a standard breakdown:

35% – cabinets
25% – labor
22% – appliances
6% – fixtures
5% – fittings
7% – other
(See worksheet under Checklists.)

One thing to keep in mind when doing your cost breakdown is that DIY (do it yourself) is not always cheaper. If you don't have the knowledge, you could end up paying between 10% - 40% more. So don't DIY unless you know what you are doing because sometimes mistakes cost more than hiring a contractor the first time. There's nothing worse than having to encore the cost of purchasing the material twice because it wasn't done right the first time.

Budget for the unexpected

When renovating a kitchen in an older home, be prepared for unexpected expenses to come up. Once you start removing walls and flooring there can be many surprises such as out-of-date electrical wiring, mold or mildew, etc. When creating your budget allow for a 10% - 20% buffer for the unexpected, this extra allowance is used more often than not.

When you find yourself in a situation where a problem has arisen and a big choice has to be made, it pays to keep a level head. Give yourself at least a day or two to make a decision on how to move forward. From my experience I have found that some people tend to rush into a decision when they are pressed for time regretting the outcome at the end of the day.

Creating a spreadsheet and checking it often will also help you ensure your budget is on track. By doing this you can make changes as needed, without worrying about going over budget.

Prioritize

When creating a budget it is very important to prioritize your wants and needs. This way if something unexpected comes up when building or renovating your home it will become clearer where you should spend your money. Countertop material, for example, can be a big expense so you can prioritize if you want granite or need granite when laminate would be a more cost effective choice this decision can really make or break your budget. (Refer to chapter 8 for more information on countertop material.)

CHAPTER SIX

Universal Design

The concept of universal design states that your home should be accessible to all people, regardless of their age, size, or ability. Successful universal design can only occur when we truly understand how people with disabilities engage in their location. Designing better accessibility is not a new way of designing, it's simply more focused on the end user.

The biggest challenge in the creation of a universal design kitchen is usually in its execution. The easiest way to guarantee that a kitchen gets built correctly is to use detailed drawings completed by an experienced kitchen designer. The end user should be involved all the way through planning, and you should set up mock ups to experiment during the process.

A kitchen is the most difficult space to make universal, and designing for minimal effort is an important concept. The kitchen should be comfortable and safe with the space being as simple and natural as possible for all family members. Everyone from a child to a senior with limited mobility should feel comfortable using the space.

A very savvy solution to universal design is using multiple counter levels. Countertop heights cannot possibly be in one position to accommodate an individual sitting in a wheelchair and another individual standing. Adjustable height counters, sinks and cooktops can solve this problem. You can have a roll under countertop at mid-height for the dishwashing sink and one at a higher height for standing food prep, for example.

The best way to achieve this is to separate the stove cooktop and oven. The cooktop and sinks must be designed to be open underneath; this allows for a person seated in a wheelchair to be able to roll under with clear space for their knees and toes so that they are protected from the heat of the stove and hot water pipes. The wall oven must be positioned at a height reachable to all users with a side swing door. It is best to have the controls for the cooktop on the front or side for easier access. Also, ensure the sink is not too deep so the person's knees can get underneath, and use lever taps, not knobs.

For people with limited agility or mobility, a wheeled trolley can be useful for carrying food from the kitchen to the dining area. It is also nice to create a design that will allow for lowered windows to allow for a nice view.

A few years ago, I designed a kitchen for a woman with a disability and we designed the kitchen to accommodate windows between the upper and lower cabinets. This gave her more light and a nice view outside from her vantage point. It also allowed for more upper cabinet space.

Upper cabinets offer great storage space, but cannot be reached by persons in wheelchairs or who are of a shorter physique. Upper cabinets can be installed with hardware that can pull shelves out and down, allowing persons in wheelchairs to access items located otherwise out of reach. Pantries are a great way to create space and provide easier access than upper cabinets.

> **Having a pull-out countertop, also known as a drop zone, is great for meal prep.**

It is usually located near the fridge and must have strong pull-outs that can hold up to downward force such as chopping.

Using mostly drawers is a better option than cabinets because it creates easier access. Having rounded corners on the countertop is another great option to avoid hitting sharp corners.

*Special thanks to Julie Sawchuk in Blyth, Ontario, who is living with a disability and teaches and speaks about accessibility, for her valuable input.

www.juliesawchuk.ca.

CHAPTER SEVEN

Specialty Features for Kitchens

One of the best feelings after you have finished a new kitchen or a kitchen remodel is realizing that everything in your kitchen has a home. It's even better when those places are functional and well placed right where you will need them.

So how do you determine what cabinet features are actually needed when you are in the planning phase of your kitchen? Create a wish list and think about your normal day to day kitchen use and what will make your life easier. Here are some features that may work for you.

Pot filler

A pot filler faucet is a swing-out faucet on a long arm and is mounted over the stove; it folds back against the stove wall when it's not in use. The faucet is mounted high enough on the wall to provide a flow of water to a big pot of pasta or soup.

This saves you from carrying a heavy pot of water from the sink to the stove and is great for filling pots that don't fit into the sink. What a cool idea!

Appliance garage

An appliance garage houses small appliances that you often use but don't always want in plain sight. Keeping small appliances behind closed doors will reduce counter clutter and creates great storage solutions.

Corner storage

Most people prefer not to have corner cabinets due to accessibility; however there are multiple ways to turn that potential dead space into usable storage. Some of these corner options are:

Lazy Susan: this is a two-tiered carousel shelving that allows easy access to stowed items; it turns at a 90-degree angle on both sides.

They spin 360 degrees giving you more storage space in this hard to reach area.

Blind Corner units may be used as a pull-out system that comes in many different arrangements. These are usually used when a lazy susan won't work with certain cabinet layout, or simply because you prefer them.

Corner Drawers are also a popular choice and they have "L" shaped fronts. You can get units that utilize the back triangular corner of the cabinet as well. When extended fully, they can be up to 30" in depth. These are a more expensive option, but they most definitely create a WOW factor.

Pot & pan drawers

Pot & pan drawers not only house your pots and pans but are also great for plastic containers, large bowls, linen or small appliances. They allow you to get creative when designing your deep drawers like adding a divider for cookie sheets, dowel systems for plates and dishes, cubbies for cutlery or drawers within a drawer for lids and pots.

Tray storage

Tray storage is an excellent space-saver. It is vertical dividers that are useful for many different kitchenware such as cookie sheets, pizza pans, cutting boards, muffin tins, etc. These dividers are often placed in narrow base cabinets or the upper portion of tall cabinetry.

The cabinet over your fridge can be awkward as it's hard to reach and really deep. Consider putting in some dividers for storing platters and cookies sheets, and adding in a roll out to help you reach things in the very back.

Bar sink

A secondary sink can be a useful addition to a large kitchen or in a nearby pantry area. Consider a bar sink for a second prep station, an island, a butler's pantry, home theater, or basement rec room.

Roll out garbage

Roll out garbages make life so much easier by arranging a trash and recycling area in your kitchen. You don't want to put your old plastic trash bin in plain sight. Get that trash behind a door; nobody wants to see (or smell) that! A double unit for trash and recycling is what most people prefer and it only takes up 12" – 18" of space depending on the garbage you choose. Many of them are short enough to accept a top drawer. Trust me on this, get a garbage pull-out, you won't regret it!

Spice pull

We all use some spices in our kitchens. Salt, pepper, paprika, garlic seasoning, the list goes on. We accumulate spices almost every time we try a new recipe. Organizing spices in an upper cabinet can be complicated when small spice bottles are stacked together on a shelf; it can be hard to see what you have without removing the entire shelf.

My favorite spice units have tiered shelves which allow spices to be displayed so you can view everything you have when you pull the unit out.

Toe kick drawers

Think you are out of storage space in your kitchen? Think Again! To gain storage space, you usually have to give up space somewhere else. Not in this case. Under almost every kitchen cabinet, there's a void. This low, shallow cavity isn't prime space for everyday items, but it's perfect for smaller flat things such as bakeware, cleaning supplies, pet dishes and more. Use every bit of space you can in your kitchen and create extra storage space by installing toe-kick drawers under your base cabinets.

Tip-out trays

Tip out trays are a plastic or metal storage directly beneath the sink cabinet. Tip-out trays were originally designed to store items in your kitchen that quickly clutter up the sink and countertop such as sponges, scrub brushes, bottle brush cleaners.

Walk-in pantry

Having a walk-in pantry enables you to get a little more creative with your kitchen design. It reduces clutter on your countertop and some walk-in pantries may have enough room for a second refrigerator. Walk-in pantries let you get a little more creative with your organization, which means that you don't have to spend time searching through several walls of shelves to find what you need. Less time looking means more time cooking.

Soft close hinges and drawer slides

Soft close hinges and drawer slides help extend the life of your cabinets by incorporating soft close door and drawers into your kitchen, no more slamming! The benefits of soft close hinges go beyond cost cutting. The system allows for drawers and cabinets to close softly and silently. There is a reason that silence and longevity are often combined with luxury. After investing thousands of dollars in a new kitchen, you want them to last and you want to show them to their best advantage. Soft close hinges add that extra touch of elegance that somehow just isn't doable when your cabinets and draws slam shut with a bang.

Wine racks

Wine racks in a kitchen are generally used for decoration and to give elegance to the space. There are many ways to incorporate a wine rack into your kitchen design; you can place it in an upper or lower cabinet either vertical or horizontal. I find a lot of people tend to use the space over the fridge for a large wine rack or at the end of an island.

Usually it can hold anywhere to 6 – 25 bottles depending on the space and design; however, when choosing the design I would recommend picking something that looks just as good empty as it does full.

Toe kick heaters

Toe kick heaters are also known as kick space or toe space heaters. They are installed close to the floor under the cabinets taking up no space on the walls allowing for more functional cabinet space. Be sure to let your designer know that you will be using a toe kick heater so you will have enough room to insert it under the cabinets and there are also some modifications that will have to be made in the manufacturing of the cabinets to ensure you will not have problems down the road with the finished product.

CHAPTER EIGHT

Countertop Options

Your countertop selection could be one of the most important choices you have to make when it comes to your kitchen. It is important to make sure you choose the counter surface that best suits your taste, budget, level of use and overall style of your home. I find when choosing a countertop you should also consider the flooring and backsplash you will be using in the space. You don't want to choose a countertop with a busy pattern and then have a different pattern in the floor and backsplash as this will make your kitchen busy and you will not know where to look, instead of drawing your eye to one thing at a time. For example, in my experience I find if you are planning on doing a plain subway tile for your backsplash, you can get away with a busier pattern in the countertop or vice versa. Another thing to keep in mind when choosing a countertop is if you are doing a design with a white countertop on a white painted kitchen you may want to choose your countertop first before choosing the paint for the cabinetry because you have a lot more to choose from when it comes to paint and you want to ensure the whites work well together.

Granite

Granite countertops are absolutely gorgeous and to be honest it's one of my favorite choices for a countertop. Granite is a natural stone, quarried from large stone deposits found around the world. Because it is all natural, there is no one piece the same, making it very unique. When choosing your granite I would suggest going to your supplier and ask to see the slabs; this way you are able to pick the piece of stone that would best suit your kitchen and style. There may be a piece with a big vein going through it, making it a great showpiece, or you may prefer a piece with a more consistent grain pattern. Granite is a porous material therefore it is very important to make sure it is sealed properly. Well-maintained granite countertops will look amazing forever. Cleaning them with products designed for granite and resealing on a regular basis will keep the stone stain resistant.

Quartz

Quartz countertops are an engineered stone countertop that is manufactured by combining 90% of a ground natural mineral (quartz) with 10% man-made material such as synthetics, plastics and dyes. This forms a very hard surface similar to granite and depending on how the stone is grounded the appearance can give a smooth look or a more flecked appearance.

These countertops are around the same price point as granite. It is extremely durable, heat resistant, stain resistant and non-porous, providing you with a long-lasting stunning product for years to come.

Laminate

Laminate countertops are available in a wide variety of colours, textures and patterns that resemble granite, concrete, marble and quartz giving you the illusion of a solid surface countertop for less the cost. You can get different edges on the front of the countertop to make it look more like stone and then go straight back to the wall bringing your tile backsplash right to the top to give you that clean sleek look. These tops are constructed from layers of plastic that are bonded to particleboard to create a countertop surface.

Laminate is easy to install compared to a solid surface countertop because of its lightweight nature. Due to the fact that laminate is a bonded plastic it can very easily be scratched or burnt so make sure you always use a cutting board and don't lay hot pots directly on the countertop, with the right care it can last for many years.

Concrete

Concrete countertops are a popular choice for kitchens. They are more customizable and custom made than the more traditional options like granite and laminate. Concrete counters have great functionality and come in a verity of different colours, textures, shapes and size to give your countertop a WOW factor. These tops can match any design style, including traditional, modern, contemporary, and transitional, plus they are long-lasting, easy to clean and care for.

Butcher Block

Butcher block can add a warm and welcoming feel to your kitchen without breaking the bank; however, you have to make sure you are ready for the maintenance that comes with this beautiful natural wood. Oiling every six months to keep the wood protected is a must and different species of woods require different finishing oil, it's best to follow the instructions of your supplier on what oil is the best. If you maintain it regularly your butcher block countertop will age gracefully, but without the right care it will crack and become very dull. Butcher block countertop can come in many different woods such as Maple, Birch, Walnut, Bamboo just to name a few. It is constructed from straight cuts of wood bonded together into pieces that provide a strong and stable surface in your kitchen. There are three different types of butcher block.

Edge grain is the most popular used for counters because of its strength and is more cost-effective than the others. It's made by placing boards on their sides and joining them so that their long narrow edges form the surface.

Face grain is less suitable for kitchen countertops then the others because it is more inclined to mark when used as a cutting surface. It is made from boards that are laid flat, their full widths with a modernized look.

End-grain is the strongest and most expensive of the butcher block tops. It is made from small rectangular blocks assembled so that the ends are visible on the surface. It masks knife marks and is gentle on blade edges.

Acrylic solid surface countertop

Acrylic solid surface is a material that is a very sleek, seamless, nonporous and easy to clean and disinfect. It's easily repaired if scratched and can be used for backsplashes and sinks. It is also available in a wide variety of colors and patterns. Acrylic countertops can be created in any shape which is helpful when planning a different shaped island.

CHAPTER NINE

Appliances

Before starting your kitchen layout, I would suggest doing some research on appliances and decide what you would like to incorporate in your design. There are so many different types of appliances to choose from and sometimes you can't always fit everything you want in the space allotted for your kitchen. If you have some ideas of what you are looking for before sitting down with your designer, then they will be able to help you create a layout that has function and style.

Sometimes I have clients who want a cooktop, double oven, microwave and 'all fridge all freezer combo' with a trim kit but the space will just not allow for it all. So if you decide beforehand what you would like to have, your designer can suggest layouts and possibly move a window or wall to allow space for everything you want before you get too far into your renovation or new build. Planning is key!

Double ovens

Double ovens offer a main oven you can use without leaning over and a second oven for warming plates or to do some additional baking. Removing the ovens from the burners also lets you incorporate a cooktop in a kitchen island or elsewhere, allowing you to add to your design possibilities.

Cooktop and range tops

A cooktop is entirely surrounded by countertop and has control buttons or touch controls that are located on the top of the counter making it safer for families with young children since the controls are on top of the counter and more difficult for children to reach. Since they "drop-in" and you don't have to worry about opening the door to an oven, you have more flexibility as to where you can install a cooktop. You can install them in areas that may seem a little unconventional, such as on a kitchen island. Other benefits of the drop-in cooktop are that it gives you more cabinet space, and a glass cooktop is much easier to clean. However you are limited in your cooking area.

A range top is built into the countertop and the cabinet. It extends from back to front of the countertop, it is deeper and takes up more of the cabinet space and the control buttons are in front of the unit. This generates more cooking space on a range top than a cooktop. The range top is almost always gas (natural or propane) giving it a higher BTU output and also has more flexibility as you can set each burner to a low simmer or high heat. You can also get different cooking surfaces like a grill or griddle.

Ranges

Your range is the pillar of your kitchen. It bakes, broils and boils, and combines a stove and oven in one appliance. There are many different types of ranges so it's best to do some research and decide what range works best for your family. A gas range can offer a level of precision that an electronic range cannot manage.

Electric ranges are popular with many consumers because of its smooth top, plus it is easier to clean and is the simplest option when it comes to cost and install. Bakers prefer electric ovens because the heat is more even.

Dual Fuel Range provides you with the best of both worlds the precision of a gas stove combined with the even baking of an electric oven. This is a great option for people that tend to do a lot of cooking, they will typically cost a bit more but the difference is worth the cost.

Freestanding Range has finished sides and a flat back. Their size is standardized so they should fit into any standard range space. They typically have a back on them to protect your wall from any mess or heat and are usually where the oven's controls are found. They're the most inexpensive and most convenient of the range design types.

Slide-in Range don't usually have a back and the controls are located in the front. It has the benefit of looking like it's built-in but it's actually much easier to install. They're also wider on top, so there's no space left between the range and the countertop.

Refrigerators

Refrigerators, like ranges, have many options; a freestanding refrigerator is the most popular choice. They tend to be less costly and they are designed for easy rearrangement. Freestanding models come in many different widths, depths and heights and many different door style options (left hinge, right hinge or French Door, for example).

'All fridge all freezer combos' come in two separate units that usually extend to 64" with a trim kit that will give it a built-in custom look in the kitchen. These units are great for a large family and a kitchen that has a lot of wall space to work with.

Warming drawer

If you're looking for a way to keep your food hot without loss of flavor, warming drawers are great add-ons to your kitchen. Ideal for parties as well as busy households, warming drawers add lots of functionality in very little space. The warming drawer concept is sweeping across the nation and the world, due to its incredible advantages. They are an independent appliance that keeps food warm, warms up the plates and even slow cooks delicious meals.

Dishwashers

Dishwashers are no longer just considered a luxury in a new kitchen; they are more of a necessity in today's society. There are so many different types and styles of dishwashers.

Built-in Dishwashers are the most common choice in kitchen design. They can be fitted under the countertop and usually come in a standard 24" width. You can also purchase an 18" width, which are more common in apartments or smaller condos.

Drawer Dishwasher provides you with flexibility for a kitchen with space restrictions or for those people that choose to run a smaller load. These are available as either a two-drawer or single-drawer option.

Drawer dishwashers are also a better choice for people with disabilities.

Microwave

The microwave is not the most attractive appliance; however, it is a necessity these days. If you have a smaller kitchen, a great space saver would be to go with the microwave range hood combo; these microwaves can vent outside or you can go with a charcoal filter. They also come in a low profile. Other options are: microwave in base cabinet, microwave over an oven, microwave trim kit, microwave drawer, standard microwave and a microwave can also come built-in to a convection oven.

Bar fridge

There are many types of bar fridges to suit your needs whether it is to store alcoholic beverages or overflow sodas and juice boxes for the kids. They come in a variety of sizes and can be free-standing or built-in. Bar fridges are available in dual-zone units that allow one half of the refrigerator to be cooler than the other. This is a great option if you are storing a variety of beers and sodas, and then another type of beverage that will require a much different temperature setting, such as wine or certain types of liquor.

CHAPTER TEN

Finishing Touches

There is more to your kitchen than just the cabinetry, countertop and appliances, so let's talk about the finishing touches that will really bring your kitchen all together.

Lighting

There are so many kitchen lighting options to choose from nowadays, it makes it difficult for homeowners to know where to begin.

Pot lights are a perfect option for kitchens, but planning is essential. Each pot light should be 20" - 23" away from the outside of the walls so that they shine on countertops but are not blocked by upper cabinets and crown moulding. These lights will offer a good amount of general light but most likely other forms of lighting may be needed. Sometimes the cabinet over the fridge is deeper, depending on the make and model; therefore, in this area the pot lights should come off the wall approximately 36".

Your lighting really reflects the style that you are trying to portray in your kitchen. Once you determine your style, make sure you select lighting that would complement the scale of the room – from small pendants over a bar area or a large chandelier over your island. A general rule of thumb when installing pendants is they should be at least 30" - 36" inches between the countertop and the bottom of the pendant. See this image as an example:

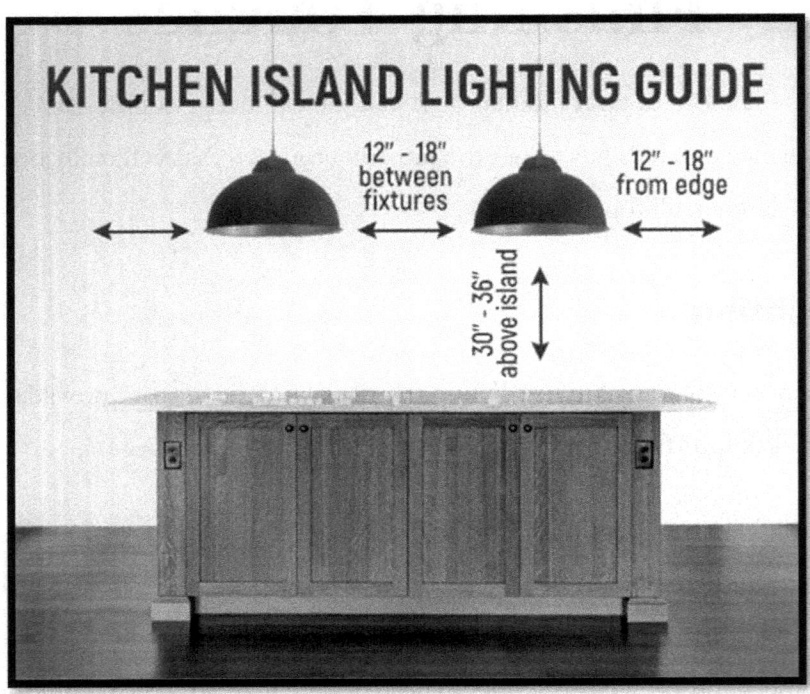

You want your lighting to look like it's made for the space. Most people try to match lighting with handle and appliance finishes but you can mix and match different metals and textures.

Standard kitchen countertops are 25 ½" deep and 13" are usually covered by upper cabinets. A great solution to getting light to where you need it most is under-cabinet lights. Just be sure to have the lighting wired in if possible, or else you will have cords hanging down and it will ruin the look of your kitchen.

Lighting in the interior of a cabinet can add softness and ambiance to your kitchen. Ensure when adding lighting to a glass cabinet you have glass shelving so the light will shine through and not just stop at the top shelf. You can also get lighting for interior cabinets and drawers that will turn on when the door or drawer opens.

Sinks

Top mount sinks or drop-in sinks are the most popular choice because they are very inexpensive and easy to install. The lip of the sink sits directly on the countertop and reduces the need for extra support. Drop in sinks are typically used when installing a laminate countertop.

Undermount sinks are the number one choice when people install a solid surface countertop (it is not recommended to use an undermount sink in a laminate countertop because these types of sinks must be glued to the underside of the counter).

Stainless steel is categorized in gauges, with a lower gauge steel being heavier and a higher gauge being lighter. Most sinks fall within the 15 to 24 gauges. The majority of residential sinks are usually between 18 and 22 gauge. 70% of all sinks are made using stainless steel. Compared to other materials, stainless steel tends to be inexpensive.

Composite kitchen sinks are made by combining 80% stone and 20% resin. This combination produces a material that is resistant to stains and scratching while still giving the same aesthetic qualities of real granite or quartz.

Single sinks are usually available in multiple sizes from compact, making them ideal for situations where space is at a premium, to a larger size which allows for easy cleaning of large dishes such as pots, oven trays, and slow cookers.

The most popular kitchen sink features two bowls. In most cases, a double bowl is ideal because of the flexibility it gives the homeowner.

Farmhouse kitchen sinks (also known as apron sinks) are often the choice for people seeking a country farmhouse design. However, there are multiple options of stainless steel and composite models that are designed to fit into a more modern design. Farmhouse sinks are available in single and double bowls, although single bowl sinks are the most common.

Faucets

When choosing a faucet, make sure the handles turn easily and special features such as pull-out and pull-down spouts work easily for you. There are no rules when picking out a faucet for your kitchen but ideally the spout should be tall enough to clear your deepest pot but not so tall that water splashes everywhere when it hits the sink's bowl.

Brass is the most popular option for a kitchen faucet because of its durability. They come in a wide variety of styles and finishes.

Stainless steel faucets are another good choice but tend to be on the more expensive side. Not to be confused with stainless-steel finishes applied over brass, solid stainless-steel faucets don't need a separate finish. If you use a well for your water supply you will find that this is a better option and will stand the test of time.

Plastic or zinc faucets are the least resilient. The best way to tell the difference is by their weight; plastic and zinc will be much lighter than brass or stainless steel.

Flooring

When picking a floor for your kitchen you have to make sure that it looks good but can handle everyday use like cooking mishaps, spills, people, and pets. So ask yourself, what look am I trying to achieve and what tailors to my priorities and budget?

There are so many different flooring options to choose from. Engineered hardwoods or natural stone tile will give you a designer look. Luxury Vinyl is easy to install and will last a very long time. Cork is great for the environment and is all-natural so you can feel good about having it in your home. Porcelain tile is reasonably priced and is highly durable. Waterproof laminate flooring is probably the flooring of choice right now due to its durability and the fact that it comes in many different styles.

Most people put the flooring down before the cabinets are installed to give a better finish and it is easier to install rather than having to cut around the cabinets. Some flooring, such as laminate, has to be installed after the kitchen.

Backsplash

For many years, a tile backsplash has been an important part of any kitchen. Besides protecting the walls, it complements the countertop as well. In today's design world we have the luxury of installing a mixture of materials like natural stone, glass, mirror, metal, brick and wood.

The backsplash is a great way to bring some of your personality into the kitchen. Traditionally when you hear of a backsplash, you think of the space between the countertop and the upper cabinets, but times have changed and everything goes now! You can install tile from the countertop to the ceiling around the window or in an area where there are no upper cabinets. You can install an accent wall over your range or you can add pops of colour to add some wow factor.

CHAPTER ELEVEN

How to Choose a Designer

Not all homeowners have the know-how to design a new kitchen. So the biggest question is how do you choose the right kitchen designer? Design errors can be very costly, so it's worth meeting with more than one kitchen designer to see who best suits you. Consider the following eight tips when choosing a kitchen designer:

1) **Design skill and creativeness**

Ask how long they have been designing kitchens and request to see some examples of their work. Will they be able to show you 3-D drawings of your kitchen design before going ahead with the project? You want a designer with an eye for how your kitchen will function in your everyday living as well. An experienced kitchen designer understands how everything fits together and why certain parts are essential. By hiring a designer, you're going to do it right the first time.

2) **Manufacturing knowledge**

Taking an empty room and converting it into a kitchen is a difficult task that needs careful planning for the new space to be a success. Your kitchen designer should have an understanding of how a kitchen is constructed in order to design a functional space. Having this knowledge will benefit you as a homeowner to make the best use of the space and will enable a custom design to fit uniquely in your home.

3) Product knowledge

Product knowledge is very important when designing a kitchen. You want to ensure you are getting a product that will stand the test of time. You don't want to go through the expense of a new kitchen to have it fall apart in a few years. Good kitchen designers will know reliable cabinet makers and the best quality materials and accessories to use.

4) Expertise

Giving your new kitchen character is what makes a kitchen remodel really special. Hiring a high-end kitchen designer is the best way to get a kitchen design that has your personality stamped all over it. A great kitchen designer will work with you to make sure your kitchen is not only functionally outstanding, but it also has a unique design to suit you and your home. A kitchen is a big investment so having an experienced kitchen designer will make your process a lot smoother and less stressful. Be sure to ask for examples of their work and check references. It's very important to ask your designer if they have a portfolio or photos of their work, not just brochures from manufacturers. Ask if they have done any projects similar to yours.

5) Understanding a client's needs and wants

If you are getting help with your kitchen remodel, whether it's a full-on kitchen design and installation service, an interior designer, or just a friend who is good at styling, be sure to stand your ground. Be confident in your choices and don't let yourself be persuaded by someone else's kitchen design. A respectable kitchen designer will have worked with various clientele and understand the importance of your input; they will essentially guide you to make the right selections for you and your home. Your kitchen designer is there to help guide you through the design process, so be clear about all the features you would like to see in your new kitchen. Kitchen designers should offer advice and assistance to help you achieve a kitchen design you are happy with. They should ask questions about your everyday life to get a feel for how you and your family functions and will want to listen to all of your ideas and concerns.

6) Communication abilities

The ideal designer-client relationship is based on honesty, trust, communication, respect, and a sense of teamwork. Make sure that your kitchen designer has good communication skills as they will be the ones dealing with building contractors, electricians, plumbers and other sub-trades to get your job done on time and on budget.

7) Testimonials

Referrals from friends and neighbors who have remodeled their kitchens are a great way to get firsthand information. Kitchen showrooms and real estate agents can also point you in the right direction. But it is also important to talk to people in the industry such as suppliers and builders; they can probably let you know if your designer responds quickly to concerns and can meet tight deadlines.

8) Credibility

Having a credible kitchen designer is very important. You want to make sure they not only understand kitchen design but also understand construction, plumbing, electrical and is up to date on all codes. Having good credibility in the industry goes a long way with builders, renovators and sub-trades.

Checklists

Types of Storage
CHECKLIST

Pantry Cabinet

- ☐ Rollout shelves for easy access
- ☐ Shallow depth for small appliances
- ☐ Adjustable shelving
- ☐ Divider for brooms

Spice Cabinets

- ☐ Pantry pullout
- ☐ Thin, filler pullout
- ☐ Spice drawer

Other Storage

- ☐ Trash, recycle cabinet
- ☐ Cabinets to ceiling
- ☐ Appliance garage
- ☐ Cutlery dividers
- ☐ Wine rack
- ☐ Glass door cabinets
- ☐ Tilt tray at sink
- ☐ Knife block

Base Cabinet

- ☐ Deep drawers for pots and pans
- ☐ Rollout shelves
- ☐ Full depth adjustable shelves
- ☐ Mixer pop up shelf

Tray Divider Systems

- ☐ In base cabinet
- ☐ In cabinet above refrigerator
- ☐ In-toe kick drawer

Corner Options

- ☐ Lazy Susans
- ☐ Blind corner units
- ☐ Corner drawers

Kitchen Remodel
CHECKLIST

Planning

- [ ] Create a timeline
- [ ] Meet with kitchen designer
- [ ] Create a budget
- [ ] Interview contractors
- [ ] Prioritize
- [ ] Make a wish list

Budget

Cabinets: $_____

Countertops: $_____

Sink/faucet: $_____

Light fixtures: $_____

Flooring: $_____

Paint: $_____

Appliances: $_____

Labour: $_____

Extras: $_____

TOTAL BUDGET:
$_____

Specifics

Cabinets
Colour:
Style:
Supplier:

Walls
Paint colour:
Backsplash:
Supplier:

Countertops
Type:
Supplier:

Flooring
Type:
Supplier:

Fixtures
Sink:
Faucet:
Knobs/pulls:

Accessories, Extras...
(write below)

Kitchen Remodel
IDEAS

Currently Works

- [ ]
- [ ]
- [ ]
- [ ]
- [ ]
- [ ]

Needs Improvement

- [ ]
- [ ]
- [ ]
- [ ]
- [ ]
- [ ]
- [ ]

Must Have's

- [ ]
- [ ]
- [ ]
- [ ]
- [ ]
- [ ]
- [ ]

Would Like to Have

- [ ]
- [ ]
- [ ]
- [ ]
- [ ]
- [ ]

Items to be Reused

- [ ]
- [ ]
- [ ]
- [ ]
- [ ]
- [ ]
- [ ]

New Items Needed

- [ ]
- [ ]
- [ ]
- [ ]
- [ ]
- [ ]

What People Are Saying About Krista Pippy

"I feel we would be doing you an unjust for not recognizing the absolutely amazing job you and your team of experts did on our new home kitchens and vanities, from the design to dealing with our needs, and changes. Your prompt delivery of our completed cabinets, which fit perfectly! But, most importantly your kind and friendly way you deal with your customers. Your installers were also amazing! Had time to answer all my questions and make me feel as I walked away that I made the right choice in selecting you. We have three more homes that we will be building in the near future. You and your team have all three guaranteed! One last thing that I did forget to mention is your pricing is very competitive, and your staff is willing to work with customers to meet or exceed their budgets when expectations are reasonable! In closing Krista, if all trades were as friendly, compassionate and simple to deal with as you, building a new home would be an absolute DREAM! You guys rock! Thank you and your staff so much! Awesome Job! See you soon for your next install! Cheers....☺"

–David Draper

"Krista has designed three kitchens for us and we were very pleased with her work. Dream Kitchens are on time and very easy to work with lots of choice. Krista will listen to what you want in a design and come back with a design you will love."

–Diane Rogers

"Thank you very much for a beautiful kitchen. Words cannot express how thrilled we are. The island is nothing less than a custom piece of furniture. Actually the whole kitchen looks like a custom piece of furniture. Many times that comment has been made by our friends. One friend described the kitchen as "truly out of a magazine". A magnificent job well done, we will recommend you to anyone looking to do kitchen renos. We look forward to you dropping by to see the finished product again, thank you from the bottom of our hearts."

—Bob and Sharon

"Thank You all very much for your excellent service. We LOVE our new kitchen. The top-notch workmanship is surpassed only by the super service. We will highly recommend your company to our family and friends."

Thank You, Cheers

—Wade and Colleen Marusiak

"I just wanted to touch base with you to say that although it's not finished yet I absolutely love my kitchen! I saw it yesterday part way through putting it together but I can already tell it is my DREAM kitchen! Thank you Thank you Thank you!"

—Christina Loveless (formerly Shortall)

"We had a good experience with your company and hope your company is successful for many years to come. Your company has shown us great professionalism and dependability. Thanks for all your help; we love our new kitchen and so do many of our friends."

—Mabel and Bob Martin

"Thank You for working with us and allowing changes during our reno project. We are very pleased with the final product. All aspects of the project went really well."

–Brenda Mackey and Ed Rogers

"I am Soooooooooooo thrilled with how the kitchen turned out! Many thanks again for your help!"

–Theresa Cook

"Adam and I just went by the house. The cabinets are absolutely gorgeous! Thank you for all of your help!"

–Jennifer

"My wife and I recently had our kitchen done by Krista Pippy. It has been a fantastic experience for us, and I'm beyond happy with everything from the consultations to the installation of our beautiful new kitchen. I'm a nervous person when it comes to these things and Krista was very attentive and met with us several times to work with us and figure things out. Our kitchen felt cramped and didn't have much storage; we had an idea of what we wanted our kitchen to be but didn't really know how to get there. Krista helped us make it real. Our kitchen was all about making the most of every inch and now the kitchen feels so much larger with way more storage. I wouldn't have thought it possible, it's amazing. Extending a cabinet here, shorten one there, move this here, that there. To look at it on paper the changes seemed subtle, but in person it made all the difference. I would also like to mention the installers. Not only am I a nervous person, but I'm also very picky when it comes to just about everything. They were exceptional and precise, way pickier than I and made sure things were just right. I stress over a lot of things; I stressed over the kitchen, each time I talked over my concerns with Krista she had the answers and made me feel at ease. When the kitchen was being installed and became a reality, I've honestly haven't been this happy about something like this in a long time. To know that if anything were to happen and needed to be fixed that Krista would be there to help make it right is comforting. She is the best. We look at our kitchen now and it's actually a little surreal, our kitchen feels like it has always been our kitchen, like it has always been this way, because it's something we've dreamed of for years. Thank you Krista!"

–Kevin Tisdale

About the Author, Krista Pippy

Krista Pippy is a part owner and the Director of Sales and Design at Dream Kitchens and Renovations. After spending 19 years designing custom cabinetry for new home builds and renovations, Krista knows what it truly takes to be successful in the industry and she can find function in any awkward space. After completing 6 renovations and 1 new home build of her own, Krista understands the latest trends, keeping in-mind the market and what the customers' wants and needs are while staying within their budget.

Krista Pippy

As a board member of the Canadian Home Builders Association (CHBA), Krista also volunteers on the Membership and Marketing Committee, and she chairs the Renovation Committee. Krista is also an active volunteer in her community, participating in the breakfast club at her children's school as well as volunteering annually at the Gower Street Church Christmas Day dinner.

Krista's two teenage girls keep her busy but she still finds time for rowing, which is one of her many passions. This is her 3rd year training and competing in various competitions. Krista's happy place is in her new home, cooking and entertaining in her gorgeous black and gold kitchen.

www.ingramcontent.com/pod-product-compliance
Lightning Source LLC
Chambersburg PA
CBHW060339050426
42449CB00011B/2794